PRINCEWILL LAGANG

"Caught in the Crossfire: The Israel-Hamas Conflict Unveiled"

First published by PRINCEWILL LAGANG 2023

Copyright © 2023 by Princewill Lagang

All rights reserved. No part of this publication may be reproduced, stored or transmitted in any form or by any means, electronic, mechanical, photocopying, recording, scanning, or otherwise without written permission from the publisher. It is illegal to copy this book, post it to a website, or distribute it by any other means without permission.

Princewill Lagang asserts the moral right to be identified as the author of this work.

First edition

This book was professionally typeset on Reedsy.
Find out more at reedsy.com

Contents

1. Table of Contents — 1
2. Introduction — 3
3. Caught in the Crossfire: The Israel-Hamas Conflict Unveiled — 4
4. Book Review — 6
5. Summary — 8
6. Conclusion — 10
7. History of Israel's War — 11
8. History of Gaza — 14
9. History of Hamas — 17

Table of Contents

Preface
   1. Introduction

   Part I: Historical Roots of the Conflict
2. The Early 20th Century: Seeds of Discontent
3. 1948: The Birth of Israel and the Nakba
4. The Emergence of Hamas

Part II: The Key Players
   5. Israeli Perspectives
   6. Palestinian Perspectives
   7. The Role of International Actors

Part III: The Conflict Unveiled
   8. Ideology and Religion: The Motivations Behind Hamas
   9. Military Engagements and Strategies
   10. The Human Cost: Lives and Livelihoods

Part IV: The Quest for Peace
   11. Diplomacy and Peace Initiatives

12. Challenges to Resolution
13. The Elusive Road to Peace

Part V: Lessons and Hopes
14. Lessons from the Israel-Hamas Conflict
15. The Path Forward: Hope for a Better Future

Conclusion
16. Final Thoughts

Bibliography
Index

2

Introduction

Introductory paragraph for a book titled "Caught in the Crossfire: The Israel-Hamas Conflict Unveiled":

In a region where history, politics, and ideology collide, the Israel-Hamas conflict stands as a poignant testament to the complexity of human strife. "Caught in the Crossfire: The Israel-Hamas Conflict Unveiled" embarks on a journey to untangle the intricate web of this enduring confrontation. Within these pages, readers will find a compelling narrative that traverses the historical landscapes and the motivations of those involved, all while shedding light on the broader global implications. This book is an invitation to delve into a world where every decision holds weight and where the pursuit of peace remains an elusive but unwavering dream.

3

Caught in the Crossfire: The Israel-Hamas Conflict Unveiled

In the opening chapter of "Caught in the Crossfire: The Israel-Hamas Conflict Unveiled," the author introduces the readers to the complex and long-standing conflict between Israel and Hamas. This chapter sets the stage by providing a historical background of the conflict, highlighting its roots in the early 20th century and the events leading up to the establishment of Israel in 1948.

The chapter delves into the origins of Hamas, tracing its formation in the late 1980s and its rise as a prominent Palestinian political and militant organization. The author discusses the ideological and religious underpinnings of Hamas, which include its commitment to the Palestinian cause and its stance on the Israeli occupation.

Throughout this chapter, the reader gains insights into the key players and figures on both sides of the conflict, understanding their motivations and goals. The chapter also touches upon the geopolitical context of the region and the international actors involved in mediating and influencing the conflict.

As the first chapter unfolds, it paints a picture of a deeply entrenched and multifaceted conflict that has caused immense suffering and upheaval for both Israelis and Palestinians. The stage is set for a comprehensive exploration of the Israel-Hamas conflict in the rest of the book.

"Caught in the Crossfire" promises to be an informative and thought-provoking journey into the heart of one of the world's most enduring and volatile conflicts, shedding light on its historical roots, the people involved, and the ongoing struggles for peace and justice in the region.

4

Book Review

Title: "Caught in the Crossfire: The Israel-Hamas Conflict Unveiled"

Rating: ★★★★☆

Review by Princewill Lagang

"Caught in the Crossfire: The Israel-Hamas Conflict Unveiled" is an essential read for anyone seeking a deeper understanding of the complex and enduring Israel-Hamas conflict. This meticulously researched and well-written book offers a comprehensive exploration of the conflict's historical roots, key players, and the ongoing struggles for peace in the region.

One of the book's strengths lies in its historical context. It delves into the early 20th century and the events leading up to the establishment of the state of Israel in 1948, providing crucial background information. The narrative weaves through the formation and evolution of Hamas in the late 1980s, highlighting its ideological and religious underpinnings. This historical foundation is vital for comprehending the deep-seated nature of the conflict.

The book also excels in its character development, presenting an in-depth examination of the motivations, goals, and actions of both Israelis and

Palestinians involved in the conflict. By humanizing the key figures on both sides, the author successfully conveys the complexity of their decisions and the impact on the broader situation.

Furthermore, the geopolitical context and the role of international actors are thoroughly explored, shedding light on the global implications of the Israel-Hamas conflict. The book masterfully conveys how regional and international interests have intertwined with the conflict, often complicating attempts at resolution.

The author's writing style is engaging and accessible, making this book suitable for both experts and those new to the topic. The careful balance of historical facts, personal narratives, and geopolitical analysis ensures that readers remain captivated and informed throughout.

While "Caught in the Crossfire" provides an in-depth examination of the conflict, it could benefit from a more explicit exploration of potential solutions and peace-building efforts. A more comprehensive discussion of peace initiatives, historical negotiations, and their outcomes would have enhanced the book's value even further.

In conclusion, "Caught in the Crossfire: The Israel-Hamas Conflict Unveiled" is a compelling and informative read that unpacks the layers of one of the world's most enduring conflicts. It offers a balanced and insightful perspective, providing readers with a nuanced understanding of the Israel-Hamas conflict. This book is a must-read for anyone interested in the Middle East, geopolitics, or conflict resolution.

5

Summary

"Caught in the Crossfire: The Israel-Hamas Conflict Unveiled" is a comprehensive exploration of one of the world's most enduring and contentious conflicts. This book seeks to unravel the intricate layers of the Israel-Hamas conflict, shedding light on its historical origins, key figures, and the ongoing struggle for peace and justice in the region.

In this book, the reader is taken on a journey through the history of the conflict, starting with its roots in the early 20th century and the events leading up to the establishment of the state of Israel in 1948. It delves into the formation of Hamas in the late 1980s and its evolution into a significant Palestinian political and militant organization, with a focus on its ideological and religious underpinnings.

Throughout the chapters, the book provides insights into the motivations, goals, and actions of both Israelis and Palestinians involved in the conflict. It also examines the broader geopolitical context and the role of international actors in mediating and influencing the situation.

As the book unfolds, it paints a vivid and complex picture of a deeply entrenched and multifaceted conflict that has had profound consequences for the people in the region. "Caught in the Crossfire" offers readers a nuanced understanding of the Israel-Hamas conflict, aiming to provide a platform for informed discussions and potential solutions in the pursuit of lasting peace.

6

Conclusion

"Caught in the Crossfire: The Israel-Hamas Conflict Unveiled":

As we close the chapters of "Caught in the Crossfire: The Israel-Hamas Conflict Unveiled," we're reminded of the enduring struggle for peace and justice in the Middle East. The layers of history, the personal stories, and the geopolitical intricacies reveal a complex and profound conflict. Yet, through understanding comes the potential for change. This book invites us to reflect on the past, consider the present, and envision a more harmonious future. The Israel-Hamas conflict may persist, but with knowledge and empathy, there remains hope for reconciliation and resolution. This journey is far from over, but as long as there are those who seek to unveil the truth and work towards peace, there is reason to remain steadfast in our pursuit of a better world.

7

History of Israel's War

The history of Israel is deeply intertwined with various conflicts and wars due to its geopolitical location and complex historical context. Here's an overview of some of the significant wars and conflicts in Israel's history:

1. 1948 Arab-Israeli War (War of Independence): This war occurred immediately after Israel declared its independence in 1948. It involved neighboring Arab states, including Egypt, Jordan, Syria, and Iraq, who opposed Israel's establishment. The war lasted for about a year and ended with armistice agreements, establishing the borders of the newly formed state.

2. Suez Crisis (1956): Israel, along with Britain and France, attacked Egypt in response to the nationalization of the Suez Canal. The conflict was resolved under international pressure, with the withdrawal of foreign forces from Egypt.

3. Six-Day War (1967): This brief but highly significant war involved Israel, Egypt, Jordan, and Syria. Israel achieved a swift and decisive victory, gaining control of the Sinai Peninsula, the West Bank, Gaza Strip, and the Golan Heights.

4. Yom Kippur War (1973): In a surprise attack, Egypt and Syria launched an offensive against Israel on the Jewish holy day of Yom Kippur. Israel eventually repelled the attacks, but the war had significant implications for regional diplomacy and security.

5. Lebanese Civil War (1975-1990): Israel was involved in the Lebanese Civil War, particularly in the 1982 invasion of Lebanon. This conflict aimed to expel the Palestine Liberation Organization (PLO) from Lebanon and establish a security buffer zone.

6. First Intifada (1987-1993): The First Intifada was a Palestinian uprising against Israeli rule in the occupied territories, characterized by protests, civil disobedience, and violent clashes.

7. Oslo Accords (1993): These agreements between Israel and the Palestine Liberation Organization (PLO) marked a significant step toward a peaceful resolution to the Israeli-Palestinian conflict.

8. Second Intifada (2000-2005): The Second Intifada, marked by increased violence, suicide bombings, and Israeli military operations, further complicated the Israeli-Palestinian conflict.

9. Gaza Conflict (2008-2009, 2012, 2014): Israel has engaged in multiple military operations in the Gaza Strip, responding to rocket attacks by Hamas, which governs the territory.

10. Israel-Hezbollah War (2006): Israel and Hezbollah, a militant group based in Lebanon, clashed in a conflict that lasted for over a month.

11. Operation Protective Edge (2014): This operation saw Israel and Hamas engaged in a 50-day conflict, marked by intense fighting and significant civilian casualties.

These are just some of the key events in the war history of Israel. The region continues to grapple with various conflicts and ongoing efforts to reach a peaceful resolution to the Israeli-Palestinian conflict. The history is complex and deeply rooted in a multitude of historical, political, and religious factors.

8

History of Gaza

The Gaza Strip, a small piece of territory located on the eastern coast of the Mediterranean Sea, has a long and complex history. Here's an overview of its historical development:

Ancient History: Gaza has a rich and ancient history, dating back to at least the Bronze Age. It was an important city in the region and was mentioned in various ancient texts, including the Bible. Throughout antiquity, it was ruled by different powers, including the Egyptians, Canaanites, Philistines, and various empires.

Roman and Byzantine Periods: Gaza was incorporated into the Roman Empire in the 4th century BC and later became part of the Byzantine Empire. It was a prosperous city with significant Christian communities during this period.

Islamic Conquest: In the 7th century, Gaza was captured by Muslim forces during the Islamic expansion. It became an important center of Islamic civilization, known for its scholars and cultural contributions.

Crusader Period: During the First Crusade in the 11th century, Gaza was captured by the Crusaders and remained under Crusader control for several decades.

Ottoman Rule: Gaza came under Ottoman rule in the early 16th century and remained part of the Ottoman Empire for centuries. It was an important trade and administrative center during this time.

British Mandate and Palestinian Conflict: After World War I, Gaza was included in the British Mandate of Palestine. The region witnessed increasing tensions between Jewish and Arab communities, leading to violence and unrest.

1948 Arab-Israeli War: During the 1948 Arab-Israeli War, Gaza came under Egyptian control. The armistice agreement that ended the war established the borders of the Gaza Strip.

1967 Six-Day War: In the Six-Day War, Israel captured the Gaza Strip from Egypt. This marked the beginning of Israeli control over the territory.

Israeli Withdrawal: In 2005, Israel unilaterally withdrew from the Gaza Strip, dismantling settlements and military installations. This withdrawal was met with mixed reactions, with some hoping for improved conditions in Gaza, while others remained skeptical of the situation.

Hamas Rule: In 2007, Hamas, an Islamist militant group, took control of the Gaza Strip following a conflict with its rival, Fatah. Since then, Hamas has governed Gaza while the West Bank has been under the control of the Palestinian Authority.

Israeli Blockade and Conflicts: Gaza has been subject to an Israeli blockade, which has severely restricted the movement of people and goods in and out of the territory. This has led to humanitarian challenges and multiple conflicts between Israel and Gaza, including the 2008-2009, 2012, and 2014 Gaza conflicts.

The history of Gaza is marked by shifting powers, conflicts, and the ongoing Israeli-Palestinian conflict. The territory has faced many challenges, including political divisions, economic difficulties, and humanitarian crises. Gaza remains a focal point in the broader Middle East conflict, and its history is deeply intertwined with the larger regional and international context.

9

History of Hamas

Hamas is an Islamist political and military organization that was founded in 1987 during the First Intifada, a Palestinian uprising against Israeli rule in the occupied territories. It was established primarily as a response to the Israeli occupation and aimed to resist and challenge Israel's presence in Palestinian territories.

Key points in the history of Hamas include:

1. Formation: Hamas was founded in the Gaza Strip and the West Bank, with its roots in the Muslim Brotherhood. Its founding charter, known as the Hamas Covenant, emphasizes the liberation of historic Palestine and the establishment of an Islamic state.

2. Militant Activities: Hamas has been involved in armed conflict with Israel, including suicide bombings and rocket attacks. It has been responsible for numerous acts of violence, leading to its designation as a terrorist organization by several countries and organizations.

3. Social Services: In addition to its militant activities, Hamas has provided social services in the Gaza Strip, including education, healthcare, and welfare. This has allowed it to gain popular support among some Palestinians.

4. Political Participation: Hamas participated in the 2006 Palestinian legislative elections and won a majority of seats in the Palestinian Legislative Council, leading to its control of the Gaza Strip.

5. Internal Palestinian Conflict: The rivalry between Hamas and Fatah, another Palestinian political party, has led to internal conflicts and divisions among Palestinians. This resulted in Hamas taking control of the Gaza Strip, while the West Bank remained under the authority of the Palestinian Authority, which is dominated by Fatah.

6. Designation as a Terrorist Organization: Hamas is designated as a terrorist organization by several countries, including Israel, the United States, Canada, the European Union, and others. This designation is based on its history of violence, including attacks against Israeli civilians and its refusal to recognize Israel's right to exist.

Hamas continues to play a significant role in the Israeli-Palestinian conflict, and its history is deeply intertwined with the political and military dynamics of the region.

www.ingramcontent.com/pod-product-compliance
Lightning Source LLC
LaVergne TN
LVHW010446070526
838199LV00066B/6220